THE TALES

JESSICA BOZEK

LES FIGUES PRESS
Los Angeles

Winner of the 2012 NOS Les Figues Press Book Contest
as selected by Sina Queryas

NOS: Not Otherwise Specified

The Tales
FIRST EDITION

Text design by Andrew Wessels and Teresa Carmody
Cover design by Chelsea McNay and Teresa Carmody

ISBN 13: 978-1-934254-50-9
ISBN 10: 1-934254-50-9
Library of Congress Control Number: 2013945225

Les Figues Press thanks its subscribers for their support and readership.
Les Figues Press is a 501c3 organization. Donations are tax-deductible.

Les Figues would like to acknowledge the following individuals
for their generosity: Harold Abramowitz, Veronica Gonzalez, Coco Owen,
Vanessa Place, Janet Sarbanes.

Les Figues Press titles are available through:
Les Figues Press, <http://www.lesfigues.com>
Small Press Distribution, <http://www.spdbooks.org>

Special thanks to: Chelsea McNay, Julian Smith-Newman, Camille Thigpen,
and Emerson Whitney.

Post Office Box 7736
Los Angeles, CA 90007
info@lesfigues.com
www.lesfigues.com

for Colleen Chandler (1953–2012), survivor extraordinaire

CONTENTS

INTRODUCTION

Jessica Bozek's *The Tales* unfolds in the aftermath of "Operation Sleep," a mysterious military mission carried out by a very powerful nation. Like the best dystopian offerings, it is composed of the actual, complicated by the intellectual and amplified by the whimsical: think Anne Carson meets *The Canterbury Tales*. *The Tales* is a disturbingly beautiful assemblage of difficult images and narratives that exist, as the poet tells us, as a record of her thinking around a seminar on "Reading Disaster."

What words does the soldier take to the front line? Or what words do we have when we become aware that the front line is now inside of us? The necessary thinking of disaster is perhaps the true province of poetry—not just in the history of American poetry but in all poetries—the song against the vanquishing night, the fairy tale as a means of warding off the demons, of keeping the children "inside" the yard.

Or, what words to take from the front lines? Bozek's tales are purportedly the tales of The Lone Survivor, but they all appear to be in the voices of people who have also survived: The Seismologist, The Actor. There are also stories from the perspective of animals—The Bird, The Dog. These brief, often Lydia Davis-style brief, tales are elegant and evocative. "The Historian's Tale," for example, which consists of nine words:

"The citizens covered their heads, sitting down to sleep." In this deceptively simple little narrative I am startled and disturbed to imagine the citizens with pie plates on their heads, frozen, like the good citizens of Pompeii, in the act of defense. The tale is both abstract and narrative, filled with character, action, and yet nothing of a traditional story, or poem for that matter. So much of contemporary poetry either wallows too much in the general wash of feelings, or tends toward stacking statistics. I am all for using language to make me see something new: here language acts like a diving board. Reading *The Tales* felt like doing roly-polys in one of those enormous clown tents. I'm far too old to be doing somersaults, but my mind is not.

Every day when I walk to my office at the university, I pass by a sign that says "Curating Difficult Knowledge…" not that I need a reminder of this. I'm not a millennial freak, but in a time devoted with such fervor to hope, faith and positive thinking, I'm constantly reminded that my mind runs to the negative. And then I feel angry about this quick and easy assessment of thinking as either positive or negative. I would rather consider an or, or, or, scenario.

I would like to say that the reason I am more concerned with air-raid shelters, emergency gadgets and stockpiling food has to do with the Cuban Missile Crisis, or living upwind of America, or that my dreams of invasion have to do with being raised during the

Cold War, or that my irrational fear of rain is about my messed up half-Catholic childhood, or that 9/11 sealed the deal on paranoia and suspicion, but the truth is it may be my relationship with language and poetry: I want language to be my emergency survival kit. I want it to wake me up. I want it, over and over again, to help me narrate my life, and then narrate it again.

Look, describe, look again, describe. I'm convinced there is something we are missing in our meander across the planet. *The Tales* reminds me of this.

Sina Queyras
Montreal
2013

THE TALES

"Everybody is supposed to be dead, to never say anything or want anything ever again. Everything is supposed to be very quiet after a massacre, and it always is, except for the birds."

Kurt Vonnegut, *Slaughterhouse-Five*

PREFACE

Once upon a recent time, a very powerful nation attempted to destroy another nation via a military mission deceptively named Operation Sleep. The very powerful nation succeeded, but for a single inexplicable survivor, known to those unmarked as the Lone Survivor. This book includes his story and many versions of what may or may not be the same story.

I.

THE REVISIONIST HISTORIAN'S TALE

"Friendly coming in!"

The soldier with the soothing voice had come. White museum booties muffled his steps. He left his weapons, the sharp and the loud ones, behind the roadside rock. Some say his whistle was distinctive.

He told the citizens stories of quiet insects of soft foods of hair-limbs of lazy of red trees of porch chairs of windrows of pinking shears of lavender of loose sleeves of a sweater that grew from trees of wind of tremor of transport of archive of crystal-glint of lunar surface of honey of typewritten notes of names going rusty from non-use of wind of wind of wind. They closed their eyes to go. And from the collective weight of so many eyelids collapsing, the pilings started to sink. They would soon be underground, the soldier would soon report that he had watched their houses retract, until low-growth covered the roofs. He whistled and their dogs followed him back to his weapons. The streetlights glistened against the greasepaint on his face.

For years afterward, people talked about the first soldier to fell a nation with bedtime stories. They wondered if it was better to be stilled into atrocity or surprised by it.

"Friendly coming out!"

THE HISTORIAN'S TALE

The citizens covered their heads, sitting down to sleep.

THE SEISMOLOGIST'S TALE

It was fall and the soldier's stories made human piles of the citizens.

He went directly to the center of each town and his stories spiraled outward. The few who tried to flee were held by his soothing voice. The citizens stopped. They grew tired and leaned. They grew tired and sat. Engines idled. They grew tired and sought other bodies to entwine with theirs. Warm slow cotton piles formed throughout the towns. The ground grew heavy.

The center of each town sunk first. The earth's tilt was perceptible only to the animals, who knew the soldier as an earthquake-maker. But this tremor moved in a different way, had a different shape. It coned. Most dogs avoided the soldier's circles, kept watch from the town's edge. Most dogs detected in the soldier's voice a sense of mission. They detected a master beyond the soldier, though the soldier had all the trappings of an alpha-human.

The leaves were thin on the trees. By the time the soldier made his final circles, only children who hadn't learned the words remained awake. Without language they felt the leaves and the leaving.

THE PULMONOLOGIST'S TALE

They didn't know they were drowning.

THE LONE SURVIVOR'S TALE

In the months that followed, I was cold. I slept with the animals, who understood that *defense* does not mean, exclusively, irrevocably, *offense*.

THE SAVING:
A FAIRY TALE

The loon's lesson.

Now under funerary green, the citizens are cut off from the surrounding lands. A loon teaches them that they can dive down into their own small lake and come up in another lake. The cost of this transport is that all communication must happen underground.

THE ACTORS' TALE

Aerial stark: a theater of shifting weather patterns, of moving currents.

We looked up and saw only the things that flew against sky—heron, helicopter, one slow leaf.

Rain falling down a heavy curtain at the end. Its drops on the ground a version of applause.

THE BIRDS' TALE

We saw it coming first, along the old road into town. Before this time, little humans on bicycles had pedaled the road's length, big humans had stopped their cars to knock bodies. The human who came that day, though, wore a dull coat. It walked a straight line along the crumbled surface, kept to the center. The trees had already grown close.

There were humans who had tried to fool us into flutter. But this human whistled differently, in rounds. We wondered, *A super-species?* Some of us followed the circles. Some humans looked up at our circles through the dusk-dark sky and grew dizzy. What accounted for the earth's give? We swooped and the humans bent below fruit trees, gripped the entrances to their nests. Our nests shook. Our young cried. When the whistling one left by the same road, the humans were nearly gone. We could hear their sleep-noises: the gurgles, the exhales, the subsiding yawns.

We swooped to grab our young in low nests. Some sang the disappearance of the human nests, their sly murdering cats. Some flew along the road, above the obedient dogs, who strode in line behind the new human.

THE DOGS' TALE

How we were suspicious.

We smelled its arrival. A bitter. We smelled it and we wanted to run for the hills. And then it spit, not caring that we could hear. Today, we knew, this new human wants to take something. We didn't think, *It wants our help*.

THE DOGS' TALE

How we were complicit.

It whistled and we didn't run. We tensed our muscles, lifted our heads. Some started toward their humans. Some readied an ambush as the word-circles widened. But pitch kept us away.

The new human wanted to leave everything. This was efficiency. The earth opened and the humans slid in. The grasses moved over them. Only we, with our collars; only we, so well-fed. We were the evidence of this population. Perhaps that's why the new human wanted us. We were trained. As it was. To sit. To heel. To eat when ordered.

THE LONE SURVIVOR'S TALE

I emerged out of the collapsed earth. My love—his hands—gone. I towed his life's work: the marionette wires, cracked wooden faces, bloody hair.

THE SAVING:
A FAIRY TALE

Air-coats.

The air was colder in the days before the soldier came, so only those with the slowest metabolisms were not wearing coats when his stories began. Many had just returned home from work or school or their secret affairs.

It is believed that beavers carry into the water so much air entangled in their coats that, if left undisturbed at the bottom of a lake, they can thrust their noses into their fur and breathe for some time. The people, of course, did not have fur, but they had winter coats.

Since the event, some villagers have been spotted coming up out of the ground.

THE NEIGHBORS' TALE

We wake in their night. We open them.

Though we slept very far off, though we slept on the other side of the lake, in another time zone, some among us claimed that the surface of the water looked like a long glassy slide, pitched toward the town of those whose bodies we now open as animals. Our children slept, though those drunk or too tired to walk were tempted by the slide.

Their hair we take, their bones. In packs we leave their organs. With organs we might understand.

THE LONE SURVIVOR'S TALE

I'm leaving messages on the undersides of leaves, so that when the others come up out of the ground, they'll know what to do.

THE SHAMAN'S TALE

I hear your mouth.

As the soldier whispered stories of wind of honey of
old trees of porch chairs of loose sleeves of long hair
of wind of warm rain of tremor of transport of archive
of eyelids of heavy moons of leisure of wind of wind,
of things the people very secretly wanted to hear, he
was exulting, *I shoot your heart. I hit your heart, oh
animals, your heart, I hit your heart.*

THE LINGUIST'S TALE

The soldier had been trained in the language of the people he disappeared. This language was a language of things and their ghosts.

The soldier wanted one thing and led the people to believe they wanted that thing, too. They were tired, and the words he used promised the simulacra of what they already knew.

His words cooed, nested—little birds straight to their sense of self. In their view, only the foreign attacked. With the soldier's guidance, the citizens believed that mutiny was superfluous. They preferred sugar, coiling, incumbent-calm.

Yet no one saw the soldier. They only heard his words. They saw their cats hide in closets, they saw their dogs slip through small flaps toward the soldier's sounds. But they, the people, were stilled by the familiar. Geologists have captured the soldier's words, but his thoughts—

THE DIAGNOSTICIAN'S TALE

Their own tongue killed them; they had too much tongue.

THE SADIST'S TALE

The soldiers came and made tunnels in the ground. The little metal mouths of their machines gnawed at the foundations of the most harmonious houses until all the citizens were disconnected, the water molecules turned disorderly, the plants wilted, and the animals' hackles were always slightly up.

On the coldest night of the year, when the stars strung their glow in the trees' upper branches, the commanding officer asked the citizens to breathe their last breath. Eager to unite once more toward some common goal, they positioned themselves across the landscape and rolled out of their skins and died.

THE LONE SURVIVOR'S TALE

In pet years, even the young ones lived to middle age.

THE METEOROLOGISTS' TALE

We did not alarm the citizens. We did not tell them, "Prepare to evacuate. A storm, the heaviest we've seen in years, is making its way to your country."

Our radar did not register beyond the tactical screen constructed by the soldier and his company. Thousands of strips of metal fogged our observation networks. For hours, we had no reading. An intern first noticed the absence of weather over this particular area on the map. We put a call in to the engineer. In the meantime, we didn't worry, in fact were charmed that an area might assert its anonymity the way some assert autonomy. The engineer was having gum work that afternoon. A matter for the next day, then.

There was an occluded front passing in one direction, a high pressure system moving into another. A normal weather day. We were happy to catch up on our work, to eat birthday cake for a month's worth of birthdays in the break room.

We lost the sky for a few hours; those citizens, though, lost it forever.

THE SAVING:
A FAIRY TALE

Controlling the sky.

In anticipation of the country's 200th anniversary, the Weather Reconnaissance Squadron began directing artillery shells at the storm clouds. It was important to understand how to force precipitation from the clouds well before the day, with its schedule of nationalistic puppet shows and fireworks in forms approximate to the country's most famous forebears. During the weeks of testing, some towns registered complaints that other towns had ended up with their rain. This meant that some towns would have prettier flowers and thus would be more likely to appear in photos commemorating the event.

The Squadron's final trial happened on the evening of the soldier's storied assault. No animal or human heard his words above the wash of heavy rain and hailstones. When the storm had passed, the country's citizens awoke to partly cloudy skies, a national birthday, and a newfound appreciation for the fruits of weather modification.

THE FIREWORKS
ENGINEER'S TALE

Pyrotechnics illustrate power. The power of a country to keep its citizens enthralled and in thrall. The power of a country to flaunt an impression of its own place in the world. The power of a country to fuck with another country.

Though it's unlikely the Lone Survivor will be watching the holiday fireworks this year, he might more readily accept his attackers' dominance if he sat down and beheld the fiery bursts: squealing pig cake, horsetail, willow, mine.

THE SAVING:
A FAIRY TALE

Like fire.

One line of thought went: *if we are to die, let us die by our own potential.* Another went: *if we are to die, let us combust, let it be spectacular.*

The citizens made themselves look like fire so that the soldier would keep his distance. It was already their habit to throw off sparks when agitated, though the youngest children could not spark. Adults threw off extra sparks to ignite the children's clothing. Flames drowned out the soldier's fatal whimsy.

(This is not a fantasy of rescue but of appropriation.)

II.

"By drilling down…we were able to extract their last breaths, piercing with a sharp metal straw the tiny crescent-shaped sac of air forced out of their lungs as they collapsed under the weight… This air…can sometimes reveal the Missing Person's final thoughts."

Matthew Derby, *Super Flat Times*

THE LONE SURVIVOR'S TALE

Nearly everything is woods now.

Outside of my house, I unspool the words of those lost:

this sadness

like a small animal

motif on wallpaper

this memory card

insects drunk in the air

hold my hand

under the heavy lights

the breath

shut up

before the breath
stopped

wedding of

limbs & limbs

thank you for sitting tight
before the fire

alarms ignite

our globules, our stains
the bumps on head, neck, arms

her hat on the floor, a plate of fried yucca

where are the sirens?

at home
under the home

who will play hero?

you ask the wrong

birds

questions

on their mid-sections

our stretch with without

through compassion or capture

what is other

we will make
our own

the enemy is often

a metonym

your freckles

sinking

myself for weeks

is it really so

arbitrary what

comforts us
compels us

to give up bed-clothes

for floor
scarred & hard

wood against all our skin

III.

THE ARCHAEOLOGIST'S TALE

What the soldier left.

Computers, bicycles, family photographs, pet birds, diaries, plates of half-eaten food, threadbare pajamas, little boxes of extra buttons, travel guides, chopsticks, game systems, power tools, picture books, flowering plants, bank cards, trophies, underthings, new toothbrushes for future guests, cleaning supplies, combs with hair stuck to the teeth, the current day's newspaper open to the crossword, an afghan made by someone's mother, cigarette lighters, holy books, freezers of meat, sweaters with holes in the writing elbow, muffin tins, junk mail, wine cellars, open notebooks, pocket knives, commemorative goblets, old batteries and light bulbs, handmade aprons, half-strung guitars, last summer's preserves, watering cans, obsolete phones and their chargers, finger paintings on the refrigerator, holiday decorations, monogrammed towels, prescription drugs, coffee grinders, running shoes, lotions for dry skin, balms for chapped lips, gels for frizzy hair, salt shakers, pruning shears, terrariums, candlesticks, shopping bags on hooks, unpaid bills, playing cards, drawers of winter clothes, decorative pillows, snack foods, sports equipment, dog leashes, cat boxes, rodents in cages, spare keys, dull scissors, umbrellas, vitamins, mixing bowls, dictionaries, souvenir keychains, suitcases, slipcovers, bath scales, unwashed takeout containers, shoe polish, spice racks.

And the owners of these things.

THE SAVING:
A FAIRY TALE

The healers' tale.

After archaeologists laid out the complete skeletons, we read the stories of the victims' lives in their bones.

Those who had been spiteful in their time lacked cartilage and connective tissue. Their bones could not be put back together.

But we stroked the clavicles of those who had been mindful and mindfully ambivalent, and they came to life once more. We gave each a pair of shoes so that the wearer might cross a mile of ground with every stride and never again be caught.

THE LONE SURVIVOR'S TALE

The government has tried to recreate my life. They've given me an office, though there are no other employees or any patients to treat. I work alone. I don't-work alone.

My voicemail message says, "Hello. You have reached the Lone Survivor. Unless you are dead, do not leave a message."

They've given me a new house, too. The distance between my new house and my new office is precisely that of the distance between my old house and my old office.

I never learned to drive, so the government runs a bus between my house and office. The bus driver wears dark glasses and a hood. She is the only person I see each day.

The government never anticipated having anything but records of the dead. There was no *What if?* No *How do we make a life that isn't worth living?*

Food arrives daily in packages I don't understand.

THE ARCHITECT'S TALE

There's a dishonesty in rebuilding. I would have made a shelter from thick paper tubes, insulated with what scraps we could find, a thick plastic tarpaulin stretched tight across the top. A true refugee structure. One that wouldn't attempt to persuade the Lone Survivor that he is living the same life, one that wouldn't remind him—by its empty chairs, clothes in the closets, and water bowl on the floor.

THE LONE SURVIVOR'S TALE

My practice was small. I listened to children's lungs and to their parents' fears. I created characters for the antigens I'd inject into older children according to the timetables.

The waiting room was decorated with felt raindrops in aqua and pink and orange. I wanted my patients to learn that meteorological phenomena are simply distinctions, without moods or value judgments.

Each examination room was named for a bird—meadowlark, hermit thrush, grackle, house finch—because birdsong is clear after rain.

THE LONE SURVIVOR'S TALE

Now, who can I heal?

THE PUBLIC RELATIONS
CONSULTANT'S TALE

They keep the Lone Survivor alive as specimen. On field trips, their children visit the New Permanent Demonstration of the Untenable Existence of Destroyed Peoples at the State Museum for the Justification of Military Action. The teachers use their pointers and speak sternly. The children yawn, but at night and for weeks to come, they wonder about the man who lives alone on this 3.2-mile tract. The brave ones vow to return at night.

THE VOYEURS' TALE

Through the windows of his house, we located the Lone Survivor. He stood working at an easel, in an orange sweater. As if he were trying to keep someone away but draw someone else near.

The walls around him swarmed with paintings: of the same two cats in different settings, groups of people, a small man with freckles under his eyes, that man's finely boned hands. The hands alone and the hands manipulating marionettes whose mouths were smeared open.

THE LONE SURVIVOR'S TALE

Hands tell the only story I can control: a painted lament for my lost puppeteer.

THE LONE SURVIVOR'S TALE

I shed clothes in remembrance. The braided cables on my sweater unravel from the neck as I wind through the tree trunks, making a cyan tangle. When there is little left, I bite down to keep the cuffs.

THE WORKERS' TALE

In the ginger rooms at Comfort Industries, workers have been given a single task they may carry out according to their talents.

The botanically inclined among them harvest rhizomes from the rows of ginger pots in filtered sunlight. Cobblers sit at a long table and stitch slipper soles from peel. And in a small kitchen, cooks strain fiber from syrup, simmering for lozenges and chews.

Assigned to console the Lone Survivor, they send him packages of their handiwork weekly.

THE LONE SURVIVOR'S TALE

Fuckers.

THE LONE SURVIVOR'S TALE

The government that did this is prepared to offer me reparations. I have so many problems with their language.

THE LONE SURVIVOR'S TALE

Does the world want to hear of my unalterable
bitterness, or my relief that I will never have to take
a strep swab again, or my inability to stop feeding the
cats I lost that evening, or the way I touch what I find
in the dirt—plastic buttons, scraps of winter-weight
wool—or, maybe, of my moving on?

THE CLAIMS ADJUSTER'S TALE

And what if the Lone Survivor wants a child? The Total Loss Replacement clause in his contract applies only to pets and human appurtenances. Pets are to be replaced according to the following criteria: species, breed, size, color, temperament. Even if the Lone Survivor did not have a pet, he is entitled to one as a "reasonable damage."

THE LONE SURVIVOR'S TALE

I did, in fact, have two cats, but I haven't revealed this to the claims adjusters who seem so concerned with fixing the physical terms of my prior life.

On the property damage claim, I may say, instead, that I had a dog of such uncertain origin that I'll accept any brown thing between 30 and 50 pounds.

THE SAVING:
A FAIRY TALE

Trying their birds.

Now they wish to become birds of flight. Sometimes they used to try this, and sometimes the birds were something.

In this version, the birds are understory birds, but they have a strength beyond their size.

THE LONE SURVIVOR'S TALE

I have begun weaving nests from the fallen hair on the floorboards and furniture. I leave these nests on high things outside. I want to be useful to the birds.

THE LONE SURVIVOR'S TALE

Jeans, two pairs. Trousers, three. Sweaters, cotton and wool and cashmere blends. Pajamas. Dress shirts, t-shirts, running clothes. A canvas trench. Some smaller things: socks, underwear, scarves, ties.

This is the pathetic list I came up with on my visit to the Garment Maker, one cog in the Total Loss Replacement machine. How could I have overlooked colors, patterns, notions? By forgetting the *things* that adorned my love's life, could I better remember *him*?

Weeks after the clothes are delivered, I open the closet, now "his" by virtue of its replicated contents. I would try these things on—to walk in his smell—but the Garment Maker has given me only the shell of him, undyed fabric ghosts to drape or hang.

THE THERAPIST'S TALE

The Lone Survivor says to me, "Some person has injured my life." I say to the Lone Survivor, "You have injured your life. Only you can fix your life."

THE LONE SURVIVOR'S TALE

I draw his eyeglasses, our best meals, his fingers working floss into the grooves between his teeth.

I keep a diary. I get bogged down in the details.

Old shoes, a bare light bulb: I take pictures of my feelings and believe I have trouble getting past the literal.

I am building up my muscles now. I outline with a purple marker the sweat stains I've transferred to the floors on which I perform my repetitions.

I am trying all of the therapeutic arts.

THE LONE SURVIVOR'S TALE

Those in charge have asked me to devise a memorial. I quickly reject statues, obelisks, all forms monumental in their ideology. Worse still, I imagine children visiting a memorial museum to experience sensory simulations of atrocity or to reenact victimhood bodily.

I consider, instead, a constellation of small clothes, each with the name of one dead inscribed on a pocket or along a hem. These clothes I would string through a woodland and arrange by meaningful adjacency. A woman's name might flutter near her partner's, their children's, her co-workers'.

I need a memorial that will disintegrate over time, gray and fray as most of the dead did not have a chance to.

THE SEAMSTRESSES' TALE

We took stores of remnant fabric and sewed clothes for the dead—simple dresses and pants, sized according to our scraps. From the garments' raw insides, blue and gray and green threads trailed.

We hung the clothes from branches. An apprentice gathered leaves from the ground and attached them with a quick backstitch. We watched the layers of muslin arms, yellowed skirts, and calico legs swell and flatten in the wind. We lost count.

Eventually, some birds took portions for their nests. We liked the metaphor of it.

NOTES

Many of these poems exist as a record of my thinking around a seminar called Reading Disaster that I've been teaching and revising for the past few years.

I first became acquainted with the heart-stopping simplicity of the Midē songs and picture-songs through Jerome Rothenberg's *Technicians of the Sacred* (University of California Press, 1968). I discovered additional picture-songs, by the Ojibwa Indians, in the second volume of *American Poetry: The Nineteenth Century* (ed. John Hollander, Penguin, 1993), which indicates as its source *A Narrative of the Captivity and Adventures of John Tanner During Thirty Years Residence Among the Indians in the Interior of North America* (ed. Edwin James, 1830). The following revise and/or appropriate language from Tanner's translations: "Preface" note, "The Historian's Tale," "The Saving: A Fairy Tale (The loon's lesson…)" "The Saving: A Fairy Tale (Air-coats…)," "The Neighbors' Tale," "The Shaman's Tale," "The Diagnostician's Tale," "The Saving: A Fairy Tale (Like fire…)," "The Saving: A Fairy Tale (Trying their birds…)," "The Therapist's Tale."

"Preface": From *OPERATIONS ORDER 17-03: Operation Sleep:*

> *Enemy Disposition:* The targets must expect, from time to time, to be hunted and killed. As long as we choose a speedy and merciful method, they should make no resistance.

> *Friendly Disposition:* The soldier's heart must be given to his business for at least two years. The soldier is always awake.

Intent: We come to change the appearance of the ground.

Concept of the Operation: It should be remembered that the language of the soldier's stories is commonly that of distant allusion, rather than direct figure; hence, though the words may seem unmeaning to us, they always convey much signification to the targets.

"The Revisionist Historian's Tale" incorporates language from "'Don't be Surprised if the Soldiers Show No Compassion At All': Anatomy of a Night Raid on Balad, Iraq," Ben Granby (*CounterPunch*, February 20-22, 2004).

"The Pulmonologist's Tale" is for Ole.

"The Lone Survivor's Tale (In the months that followed…)": Howard Zinn noted, in "Beyond the War in Iraq," a talk he gave at Boston University on November 6, 2007, that the United States has not been involved in a defensive war for about a century. Our Department of Defense would more accurately be called a Department of Offense.

"The Sadist's Tale" and **"The Saving: A Fairy Tale (The healers' tale…)"** adapt details from Ojibwa and Odawa fairy tales. See "The Star Maiden" and "The Adventures of the Living Statue" in *American Indian Fairy Tales* (Margaret Compton, 1907). Additionally, "The Sadist's Tale" draws on a theory presented in the (pseudo-scientific?) documentary *Water: The Great Mystery* (Saida Medvedeva, 2008)—that water reflects emotions projected onto it via changes in its molecular structure.

"The Meteorologists' Tale": Frederick Taylor, in *Dresden: Tuesday, February 13, 1945* (Perennial, 2004), describes the

Allied bombing of Dresden and the screen that allowed 244 Avro Lancaster bombers, each "big with a seven-ton load of bombs and incendiary devices," to reach Dresden undetected: "they... pass beyond the protective shield of 'Mandrel,' the jamming screen...to fog the enemy's radar defenses. 'Window' devices are dropped in the thousands to further confuse the enemy. En masse, these small strips of metal appear on German radar screens as a wandering bomber fleet while the real aircraft do their work elsewhere" (4).

"The Saving: A Fairy Tale (Controlling the sky...)": I first became aware of the phenomenon of "cloud-seeding" when I lived in Russia in 1998. The sky looked ominous on the morning of Victory Day, when Russians celebrate their victory over Nazi Germany. Rumors abounded that the clouds would be shot to ensure a clear sky during the parade and fireworks. Whether or not this happened, it never rained that day. More recently, China used cloud-seeding to ward off storm clouds during the opening ceremony of the 2008 Olympics in Beijing. Weather modification has also been used to increase precipitation for agricultural purposes and to decrease air pollution. The practice is controversial and generally dismissed by scientists in the United States and Australia. China, however, continues to expand its cloud-seeding program. Of tangential note: Kurt Vonnegut's brother Bernard Vonnegut was one of the General Electric scientists who discovered the weather-modification potential of silver iodide in the 1940s.

"The Lone Survivor's Tale (The government has tried...)": In "Casualties of War," from *Better: A Surgeon's Notes on Performance* (Picador, 2007), Atul Gawande writes about the impact of trauma care on injured American soldiers in Iraq and Afghanistan: "We have never faced having to rehabilitate people with such extensive wounds. We are only beginning to learn what to do to make a life worth living possible for them."

"The Architect's Tale": Japanese architect Shigeru Ban spoke about his work constructing temporary refugee houses at the Museum of Fine Arts, Boston, on April 28, 2010. Additionally, George Packer discusses the very different approaches to rebuilding that Berlin and Dresden have taken since World War II in "Embers," published in *The New Yorker* (Feb. 1, 2010). Packer refers to Dresden as "the Blanche DuBois of German cities—violated, complicit in its violation, desperate to recover its innocence," in large part because of efforts to restore the city's buildings to their former grandeur, with little acknowledgment of the 1945 firebombing. Berlin, by contrast, "can seem an overly earnest therapy patient in its insistence on showing visitors the full array of its crime scenes and self-inflicted wounds."

"The Lone Survivor's Tale (Now, who can…)": This poem pays homage to W.S. Merwin's stunning "Elegy," the single line "Who would I show it to."

"The Lone Survivor's Tale (I shed clothes…)" is based on a pair of small Francis Alÿs paintings I saw at the Philadelphia Museum of Art. However, the museum must not have these paintings any longer, and I can't find any evidence that they exist. It seems that Alÿs also enacted the unraveling in a series of public actions called Fairy Tales in the mid-nineties. I do not know whether the paintings of a man in an unraveling sweater precede Alÿs's unraveling of actual sweaters.

"The Lone Survivor's Tale (I did, in fact…)" is for Clem.

"The Lone Survivor's Tale (Jeans, two pairs...)" references the replicators in Chris Adrian's *The Children's Hospital* (McSweeney's, 2006).

"The Lone Survivor's Tale (Those in charge...)": In determining how to display victims' names as a part of Michael Arad's 9/11 memorial Reflecting Absence, the foundation in charge of The National September 11 Memorial & Museum solicited "meaningful adjacencies" from victims' families (i.e., connections that reflect work cohorts, family bonds, and friendship). Artist and designer Jer Thorp created the algorithm to deal with these adjacencies. Source: Nick Paumgarten, "The Names" (*The New Yorker*, May 16, 2011).

Paul Williams, in *Memorial Museums: The Global Rush to Commemorate Atrocities* (Berg, 2007), defines memorial museums as those "dedicated to a historic event commemorating mass suffering of some kind." Susan Sontag, in *Regarding the Pain of Others* (Picador, 2003), disparages "the marketing of experiences, tastes, and simulacra" by some museums, including the Imperial War Museum in London, with its "two replicated environments": "from the First World War, *The Trench Experience* (the Somme in 1916), a walk-through complete with taped sounds (exploding shells, cries) but odorless (no rotting corpses, no poison gas); and from the Second World War, *The Blitz Experience*, described as a presentation of conditions during the German bombing of London in 1940, including the simulation of an air raid as experienced in an underground shelter" (121). Germany's new Dresden Museum of Military History, opened in 2011, promised to go even further: "visitors will be able to inhale the smell of death from the trenches of the First World War" (Packer).

The Lone Survivor's idea for a memorial is something of a counter-monument, a concept I learned about via Jochen Gerz and Esther Shalev-Gerz's Monument against Fascism, created in Harburg, Germany, in 1986. The inscription at the base of the monument reads: "We invite the citizens of Harburg, and visitors to the town, to add their names here next to ours. In doing so we commit ourselves to remain vigilant. As more and more names cover this 12-metre tall lead column, it will gradually be lowered into the ground. One day it will have disappeared completely, and the site of the Harburg Monument against Fascism will be empty. In the end it is only we ourselves who can stand up against injustice." Between 1986 and 1993, the monument was lowered eight times. Over 70,000 signatures were inscribed onto its surface. Some respondents left neo-Nazi graffiti, which only amplified the need for citizens to commit themselves to being vigilant against fascism, the monument's intention after all.

"The Seamstresses' Tale": The immediate influence for this idea comes from Anselm Kiefer's paintings and sculptures that incorporate flattened nightdress-like garments. For example, *Die Himmelsleiter* (1990) and *Die Himmelspaläste* (1997). Charles LeDray's work is considerably less sinister, but bears mention, as LeDray, too, works with clothes. In *workworkworkworkwork*, his 2010 exhibition at the Institute of Contemporary Art, Boston, LeDray displayed countless hand-sewn garments, each a miniature version of an original, sometimes with an even more miniature version cut out of and created from the already miniature version.

ACKNOWLEDGMENTS

My sincerest thanks to the editors of the following journals, where some of these poems first appeared, at times in different forms and with different titles: *751, Action, Yes, Artifice Magazine, Black Warrior Review, Guernica, Horse Less Review, Sawbuck, Sixth Finch, The Volta,* and *Womb.*

"The Lone Survivor's Tale (In the months that followed…)" was published as a limited-edition coinside by Brave Men Press (2010).

I would like to thank Sina Queyras for selecting this book and the folks at Les Figues for their support. *The Tales* might not exist without my Reading Disaster students at Boston University. Thank you to them for the opportunity to think about and discuss many of the texts informing this one. I also owe a huge debt to my writing group for bearing with these poems for three years; Carrie Bennett, Amaranth Borsuk, Cheryl Clark Vermeulen, Kevin McLellan, and Anna Ross, I am so privileged to have first dibs on your reading attention. Thank you to Eli Queen, who always has the right idea, long before I know it's the right idea. And, finally, thank you to Anja Bozek Queen, whose approaching arrival propelled me to finish this book.

THE AUTHOR'S TALE

Jessica Bozek is the author of *The Bodyfeel Lexicon* (Switchback, 2009), as well as several chapbooks: *Squint into the Sun* (Dancing Girl), *Other People's Emergencies* (Hive), *Touristing* (Dusie), and *correspondence* (Dusie). She runs the Small Animal Project Reading Series and lives with her small family in Cambridge, MA.

ALSO AVAILABLE FROM
LES FIGUES PRESS

Words of Love Mark Rutkoski

The Field Martin Glaz Serup (trans. by Christopher Sand-Iversen)

Guantanamo Frank Smith (trans. by Vanessa Place)

Chop Shop Stephanie Taylor

A Happy Man and Other Stories Alex Thormählen (trans. by Marianne Thormählen)

The New Poetics Mathew Timmons

Our Lady of the Flowers, Echoic Chris Tysh

Things To Do With Your Mouth Divya Victor

2500 Random Things About Me Too Matias Viegener

The nOulipian Analects (eds. by Matias Viegener, Christine Wertheim)

+l'me'S-pace Christine Wertheim

Feminaissance (ed. by Christine Wertheim)